Jesus the Disabled God

Jesus the Disabled God

JENNIFER ANNE COX

RESOURCE *Publications* · Eugene, Oregon

Resource Publications
An Imprint of Wipf and Stock Publishers
199 W. 8th Ave., Suite 3
Eugene, OR 97401

www.wipfandstock.com

PAPERBACK ISBN: 978-1-5326-3454-3
HARDCOVER ISBN: 978-1-5326-3456-7
EBOOK ISBN: 978-1-5326-3455-0

Manufactured in the U.S.A.   AUGUST 8, 2017

To the people of Christian Blind Mission,
who demonstrate the love of the disabled God every day
by transforming the lives of people with disabilities
in the poorest nations of the world.

Contents

Introduction

D URING 2005 I BEGAN to think about disability from a bibli-
cal perspective. This interest was sparked by the fact that two
of my children have (different) disabilities. I was unable to make
sense of these disabilities and needed to know what the Bible had
to say. While some people come to grips with their problems by
keeping a journal or writing poetry, I do so by thinking about how
they make theological sense. My search for answers first led me to
read through the Bible, looking at different disabilities. In my quest
for understanding I decided to consider disability while studying
theology. This short book is a heavily revised version of an honors
thesis that I wrote while completing a Bachelor of Theology.

There are several questions that I am trying to answer in this
book. Does God care about people who live with disabilities? How
could God know what it is like to be disabled? Will people have to
live with their disabilities forever? The Bible has a lot to say about
disability in both Old and New Testaments. But here I have focused
on the person and life of Jesus. It is in Jesus Christ that we meet the
God who became a human being. Jesus has revealed God to us in
himself, his life, his ministry, his death, and his resurrection from
the dead. If we are to understand God's concern for people with
disabilities, then looking at Jesus is the best place to begin.

The way in which I will explore the questions I have asked is by examining four aspects of the life of Jesus: his incarnation, his ministry, his death, and his resurrection. Jesus did not begin to save humanity on the cross. Rather, his entire life is redemptive. From the moment the Virgin Mary was made pregnant by the Holy Spirit until Jesus was raised from the dead, Jesus acted to save humanity by fighting against all the spiritual forces that oppose us. Every aspect of the life of Jesus is one in which he worked from within the human experience to save humanity. And yet the cross is the center of this book because the cross is emphasized by the Bible as the point at which Jesus bore the sins of humanity.

I have titled this book *Jesus the Disabled God* because Jesus has demonstrated his concern for people with disabilities by becoming disabled himself on the cross. I am not the first person to write about Jesus as the disabled God. *The Disabled God* is the title of a book by the late Nancy Eiesland. She believed that Jesus is the disabled God because after he was raised from the dead he still has the scars of crucifixion in his hands, feet, and side. "The Disabled God" is also the title of an article by Burton Cooper. My ideas differ from both Eiesland and Cooper because I make different assumptions about Jesus and about the nature of God. In particular, I believe that Jesus is not disabled in his resurrected state and that God does not experience disability in eternity. Jesus is the disabled God because of what happened in his earthly life and ministry, but he is now risen and does not experience disability any more.

I write as an evangelical theologian, so I believe that the Bible is the word of God in written form. It is true in its entirety and it faithfully records the life and teachings of Jesus. The Bible is a book that provides us with what we need to understand God and to live lives that are godly. Because of these assumptions I have begun with the Bible, rather than with the experience of disability. However, I have taken the experience of persons with disabilities seriously and interpreted those experiences in the light of Scripture. I have adapted many common themes of evangelical theology relating to the life of Christ and applied these to disability.

Throughout this book I have assumed several things about disability. First, I have assumed that having a disability involves some kind of suffering, whether this is discrimination, pain, frustration due to inability, or shame and stigma. Often people writing about disability have downplayed the issue of personal suffering for persons with disabilities, preferring to see disability as a matter of discrimination or lack of accessibility. While not denying that many difficulties for persons with disabilities are socially imposed, having a disability also involves some personal suffering, which could not be removed even if no discrimination or access issues existed.

A short word is needed in regard to terminology. "Persons with disabilities" is the term most often used by the disability rights movement to designate those who have disabilities. I have followed this practice because people who have a disability are not defined by that disability. People with disabilities are first and foremost people for whom Christ died. In addition, people with disabilities are people with interests, relationships, desires, and hopes. Disability is only one aspect of their lives and not the whole of their lives. I have also used "persons with intellectual disabilities" to describe people who have an intellectual rather than a physical disability. Disability refers to more than being unable to do something. Having an impairment means that a person may be unable to perform a certain function. The impairment becomes a disability when society refuses to make an accommodation for the person with that impairment. So being unable to walk is an impairment. This becomes a disability when there are no ramps for wheelchair users to access buildings.

There is much more that could be said about disability and the Bible, or disability and God, than I will say in this book. Mental illness is often considered to be a form of disability, but consideration of that topic will be left for another book. I will mainly be concerned with physical disabilities, but I will touch on intellectual disability in places. My discussion of disability is a very general one. I do not focus much on specific disabilities. It is also important to remember that when I speak of Jesus being the disabled God, this is not the major focus of the New Testament. The central story of the Bible concerns God's actions to redeem humanity from the power of sin and death and to reconcile people to himself. God's concern for disability is only one aspect of this wider picture of redemption.

This short book is intended to address ordinary Christians who desire to understand disability in a theological way. I hope that it might provide hope to Christians who live with disability, either their own disability or that of a friend or family member. Although I am indebted to all the theologians whose work I have read, none of them are mentioned in this book because the theology expressed here is aimed at those who are not theologians in any formal sense.

There are four chapters in the book. Each is devoted to a particular part of the life of Jesus. The first discusses how the Son of God humbled himself and became a human being. He became human by choice, and in doing so also freely chose to experience the things that humans experience. One of those things is disability.

The second chapter discusses the ministry of Jesus towards people with disabilities. Jesus ushered in the kingdom of God and brought healing to many as a consequence. The healing that Jesus brought encompassed many different aspects of life, not merely the physical. As well as healing, Jesus also identified with people with disabilities. He became the God of the disabled.

The central chapter is about the cross. It was on the cross that Jesus became disabled himself. In doing this he truly became the disabled God. But this event was not happenstance; it was the result of Jesus' obedience to God and it was planned before time. The fact that Jesus became disabled on the cross makes a difference to how God understands disability and it should make a difference to how humans understand disability.

The final chapter considers the resurrected Jesus. He is still the disabled God, but he is not disabled any more. The resurrection provides hope for all believers because the disabled God has overcome death.

1

Jesus Emptied Himself

INTRODUCTION

PEOPLE DO NOT GENERALLY choose to be impaired or to experience the disabling effects of social restrictions. Without having this experience how can someone on the outside know what it
is like to be disabled? Since this book is about Jesus as the disabled
God, the real question here is: how can God know what it is like
to be disabled? God is all powerful and all knowing. He does not
have an impairment; there are seemingly no limitations on the life
or the abilities of God in heaven. Is it possible, then, for God to be
disabled?

In order to answer this question we must consider the possibility of God suffering. If God were to experience disability he
must suffer. Here I consider the idea that God is able to suffer, but
not that he must suffer. God is free to suffer by choice and this is
what Jesus did. The eternal Son of God chose to empty himself in
the incarnation to become the man Jesus Christ. In doing this he
became genuinely human and experienced all the sorts of things
that humans experience, including human suffering. Because becoming human exposed Jesus to the possibility of being disabled,
the incarnation is the first step for Jesus in becoming the disabled
God. And yet the decision to become human and face the possibility of disability actually occurred before the creation of the world.

DOES GOD HAVE TO SUFFER?

It is certainly true that we could not give the title of disabled God to a God who had not experienced disability. But it is equally true that anything that we say about the God of the Bible needs to be stated very carefully if we are to be faithful to what has been revealed to us. The first question that needs to be asked here is whether it is necessary for God to suffer in order to be the God he is. Does God suffer eternally? In the history of the church, no one has really asked this question until the last century. Before that Christians generally believed that God is impassible, that is, God cannot suffer. But during the twentieth century some theologians have argued that a God who does not suffer is not worthy of being called God. Others insist that a suffering God is the only means of coming to grips with suffering in the world.

The Bible gives us some good reasons for considering the possibility that God suffers. In the Old Testament, God was intimately concerned with the nation of Israel and even grieved over Israel's enslavement in Egypt (Exod 3:7). His is both a God of faithful love (Ps 117:2) and a God who expresses wrath over the sin of Israel (1 Kgs 16:2). Because this God is a God of love, involved with real people in history, some therefore argue that God *must* suffer. God must suffer because he loves. One theologian insists that a God who is unable to suffer in any way is also unable to love. According to this argument, love includes within itself the possibility of sharing in the suffering of the other.

The fact that the Son of God became human provides an even stronger argument for the suffering of God. The experience of suffering that Jesus underwent on the cross is the particular focus of these claims. The idea that God suffers is based on the fact that Jesus is both God and man in the one person. Some believe that both the human and the divine natures of Jesus suffered on the cross. It is this suffering, the argument goes, that makes God most Godlike. Certainly the person of Christ and his suffering are the right place to begin this discussion. But we do not need to come to the conclusion that God *must* suffer.

It is true that Jesus is both God and man in the one person. However, we need to be careful about the conclusions that we draw from this fact. It is wrong to conclude that when Jesus was crucified only his human nature suffered. It is also wrong to fuse the two natures of Jesus—his humanity and his deity—and make divine suffering necessary to the being of God. We should not conclude that because God is love he *must* participate in the suffering of his beloved people. Although it may have some romantic appeal to believe that God suffers eternally in solidarity with humanity, this would imply that suffering is part of God's being in the same way that love is. The result would be that when humans are glorified—when Jesus returns—they would participate in this part of God's essential nature and therefore suffer forever. This is not something that anyone would want, nor would we expect this based on what the Bible tells us.

The notion of God suffering eternally would have been abhorrent to the early church. The early church fathers did not accept that God *must* suffer. They believed that the Son of God did not suffer by nature, but only suffered during the time of his earthly ministry and death (compare Rom 8:18). Therefore, the martyrs in the early church were sure that, because they participated in the suffering of the earthly Jesus, they would also participate in the glory of Jesus, who is now in heaven. In the glorified Jesus all suffering comes to an end. Suffering is not part of God's eternal being. Instead we can say that the suffering of Christ is part of a free act of love by God.

God does not have to suffer; he does not suffer eternally. We cannot say that suffering is part of God in the way that love is a vital part of God's being. This is not to deny that God can suffer, only that if God suffers he does so because he chooses to do so as a free act of love. Since Jesus demonstrates the love of God to us, we know that God has chosen to experience suffering in the person of Christ. The difference between God suffering because it is part of his being and suffering by choice is that a God who *must* suffer cannot give hope to people who are disabled in the present.

GOD FREELY CHOSE TO BECOME HUMAN

I am arguing in this short book that Jesus became the disabled God. The question that I am trying to answer here is whether this just happened to him or whether he chose to become disabled. We have already seen that God does not have to suffer, but if he does suffer it is by a free act of love. This means that it is important to understand God's freedom. The incarnation of the Son of God, that is, his becoming human, was a free choice on his behalf. This choice opened up the possibility that he would experience disability.

God is absolutely free. He can be himself without needing anyone or anything other than himself. Nothing outside of God forces God to do anything at all. Indeed, God has no need of anything outside of himself. He is utterly complete in his being. So whatever God does in relation to human beings is the result of his free choice. God's actions towards us are not a reaction to what humans do or have done. Nor does God need creatures in order to have someone to love. He already is love (1 John 4:8) since the Father loves the Son in the Spirit (John 3:35, 5:20) and the Son returns that love. So God loves his human creatures because he already loves himself and chooses to share that love with them. When God loves us he does so freely.

What this means is that when the Son of God became the human being Jesus, this was a free act of God. Nothing forced God to become human except the decision of his own will. When the Word became flesh and dwelt among us (John 1:14), the Word was not made flesh by someone else's actions, but as a result of his own decisions. Nothing in God requires that God become human. No law exists that God is subject to and that could force him to become human. No one humbled the Son of God; he humbled himself. If this were not the case, if God were not free to choose to become human or not become human, then when the Son emptied himself (Phil 2:7), it would not be so much a sacrifice as the end of his divinity.

Yet the freedom of God includes the freedom to serve and freedom to be humble. God's freedom means that he is free to rule from heaven and also free to serve others. He is free to enter the world as one with the lowest possible status, that of a slave. He is free to be hated by those he came to serve and to be rejected by them. God is free to live in exalted glory and to be worshipped by angels. But he is also free to humble himself and to willingly die for humanity, experiencing the futility, emptiness, darkness, and abandonment that are the lot of sinners. The God who in Jesus Christ shares the plight of humanity is the God who is free to embrace poverty in order that his human creatures might become rich (2 Cor 8:9).

God, then, is in no way forced to become the disabled God. If the Son of God became the disabled God he did so freely. God freely chose to love his creatures and to humble himself in the incarnation. In the incarnation the Son of God was still free in his actions, free to serve the world, and free to die. This freedom includes the freedom to allow himself to be disabled, with all that this entails—weakness, impairment, pain, and stigma—in order to enable persons with disabilities.

WHAT DOES IT MEAN FOR GOD TO EMPTY HIMSELF?

The Son of God freely chose to become a human being. What does that action involve? Philippians 2:6–7 speaks of Jesus "who, though he was in the form of God, did not regard equality with God as something to be exploited *but emptied himself,* taking the form of a slave, being born in human likeness." The theological term for "emptied" is *kenosis,* from the Greek word *kenoō.* This leads naturally to the question: what does it mean that the Son of God emptied himself? This question has been the subject of many theological discussions. However, what we can say with certainty is that although Jesus emptied himself he did not cease to be God. On the other hand, it also means that he is genuinely human; he did not merely appear to be human.

Kenosis is clearly a complex idea. But some things can be positively and clearly stated. Although Jesus was in the form of God (Phil 2:7), he was free to put aside that form. He freely took the form of a servant, even a slave. He freely gave up all claims to the glory that was his by right. In this way he demonstrated that the God of the Bible is the kind of God who is free to give up what is his. And yet, at no point in emptying himself did Jesus cease to be God. The Son of God could not and did not renounce his own divinity. He could not be other than himself, even while being a human.

We must clearly affirm that Jesus is God, but we must equally affirm that he is a genuine human being, with all that being human involves. The early church made sure that this was emphasized since some people said the opposite. The idea that Jesus was not truly human took two different forms. In the first, Christ did not have a real human body, but only the appearance of one. According to the second, more subtle view, Christ was divided into two natures—the human nature and the divine nature—the latter of which had nothing to do with base human realities, most especially birth and death. In both these distortions the heavenly savior had nothing to do with human experiences. In contrast, the church fathers insisted that real humanity requires a real human redeemer, not a counterfeit one.

The *kenosis*, or emptying, of the Son of God is very important to the matter of suffering, and therefore to a consideration of disability. The suffering of God is not the same as human suffering. So if God is going to experience human suffering and disability, then he must become a human being. This is exactly what took place in Christ; God did become a human. The humanity of Jesus is the same kind of humanity that we all possess. He had the same form and experienced the same kind of experiences that all humans experience (Rom 1:3; Phil 2:7; Heb 2:14–15). The importance of God experiencing human suffering in Christ cannot be understated. We don't need to be assured that God as God experiences suffering, but we do need to recognize that God knows what it is like to experience human suffering as a human. This is precisely what is true about Jesus the God-man. He is God and he experienced human suffering, so he knows what we experience.

It is important to remember that Jesus is still God even in his incarnation. He cannot be the disabled *God* if he has lost his deity. But he also had to become human in order for God to experience human suffering and human disability. And that humanity had to be genuine. It would do us no good if Jesus' humanity was only a show or only involved the happy experiences in life and not the difficult ones. Without the aspects of life that are unpleasant or even plain ugly, especially suffering and death, Jesus could not save real humans, whose lives are fraught with difficulties and death. Therefore, as a genuine human being the Son of God was able to become the disabled God by becoming a person with a disability.

THE BEGINNING OF WEAKNESS

The incarnation was something new for God. Up to that point, God had not experienced what it is like to be a human. In particular, God had not experienced being weak. Being the disabled God must involve weakness, but God did not know weakness before the Son of God became the man Jesus Christ. So the weakness of the incarnation is the beginning of becoming the disabled God. It is the beginning of the process of dying, to which all humans are subject, but that God had never experienced.

The man Jesus Christ did not live as the omnipresent, omniscient, and omnipotent God. He took on weakness simply by becoming a human being. Jesus accepted all that it means to be human. He was in a world broken by sin, inhabited by sinners, and dominated by death. He did not come as the exalted Lord, but as a God who is hidden in weakness. He was lowly and poor, a man who knew that he would have to die, just as sinners know they must die. Like Israel, who lived under the wrath of God, he suffered as a man who was daily perishing under the wrath of God. This was the weakness of the Son of God.

Therefore, in one way, the incarnation is the first step to becoming the disabled God. There is, in the very fact of taking on the limitations of a human life, an impairment of divine ability. This impairment was freely taken on and it does not and cannot mean that Jesus ceased to be God, but it was a real impairment. Taking upon him a body that was subject to death was another way in which the incarnation led to becoming the disabled God. Death contains within itself the dissolution of the body, and this dissolution becomes more evident as the moment of death comes closer. As a human being with a corruptible body, Jesus took the chance of acquiring a physical disability from the moment of his conception. This is not all that is involved in being the disabled God, but it is a first and significant step.

THE SAME YESTERDAY, TODAY, AND FOREVER

Although the incarnation was something new for God, it is also true that "Jesus Christ is the same yesterday and today and forever" (Heb 13:8). What God revealed about himself in the gospel as Father, Son, and Holy Spirit, was always what God was like eternally. Before the world began, God had already decided to enter into the creation in Christ (Gal 4:4; 2 Tim 1:9; 1 Pet 1:20). The God who knew that his human creatures would sin and subsequently die decided to redeem them before time began. Jesus decided to die on the cross before the world began (Rev 13:8). In some sense the events of Calvary were part of a reality that began before creation. So when the Son of God chose to become weak, this was not a new idea, but a decision he made before the foundation of the world.

Consequently, the decision to become the disabled God did not occur after Jesus was born. It was made before there were any humans at all. When the Son of God became the man Jesus, he knew that he would become disabled at the end of his life. When he became human, the risk of becoming disabled began. But the disabled God was always the disabled God because he had already chosen in eternity to take on weakness. He eternally had a heart that wanted to deal with death, disease, and disability. This redemptive activity would not become reality until the cross and resurrection, but it was always planned.

CONCLUSION

God does not have to become the disabled God. This is clear because he does not need to suffer. If God were to suffer, it would be because he chose to do so out of love for us. And this is precisely what God has done in entering the world in the person of Christ. In becoming human Jesus Christ opened himself up to suffering in the same way that human beings suffer. The Son of God became a genuine human being. Jesus was not simply God pretending to be human without the real human experiences of birth and death. He actually experienced the kinds of things we experience. Just as every human has the possibility of acquiring a disability, from birth Jesus Christ had the possibility of becoming disabled. Because Jesus is not just human, but also God, the possibility of Jesus becoming disabled is the possibility of God experiencing disability. This was not possible for God before the incarnation. And yet it was something that the Son of God chose before time. Before the creation of the world, he had already made the decision to become the disabled God, to experience disability, and to redeem people with disabilities. The incarnation is the first step in the process of becoming the disabled God, but it was not the beginning of God's love for people with disabilities. That was eternally in his heart.

2

The Life of Jesus

INTRODUCTION

JESUS DID NOT MERELY enter into the experience of human beings and open himself up to the possibility of having a disability.
He is the disabled God because he experienced disability in the
last hours of his life. However, his attitude and his actions towards
persons with disabilities are extremely important. If Jesus is to be
rightly called the disabled God then he must not only have experienced disability, but he must have a positive attitude towards persons with disabilities. If this were not so, the significance of Jesus
becoming disabled would be considerably lessened or completely
undermined.

In this chapter I will examine the next phase in the unveiling
of the disabled God, that is, the relationship between Jesus and
persons with disabilities. Jesus met and interacted with many people who had disabilities. His ministry included healing of many
people. The healings were part of his ushering in the kingdom of
God. In the kingdom of God the whole person is healed. There
are many aspects to healing. It includes acceptance, inclusion,
restoration to community, and most certainly physical cure. Some
disability advocates believe that physical cure is not necessary for
disabilities because the important aspects of healing are not physical. Yet the fact that Jesus healed physically should not be ignored.

Jesus' attitude towards people with disabilities was positive. He had compassion on them, challenged the attitudes of his culture, restored people to wholeness, and treated people with dignity. In some ways Jesus identified with people with disabilities. He became a human in a nation that was politically oppressed, like so many people with disabilities. Every time he ministered to others it was at a cost to himself. And his ministry to those with disabilities pointed them to both his cross and his resurrection.

THE KINGDOM OF GOD

It has eternally been in the heart of God to become incarnate and to liberate humanity. The healing miracles of Jesus are also part of God's eternal plan. The New Testament describes the execution of this plan as the arrival of the kingdom of God (Mark 1:15; Luke 4:43). Jesus' healing ministry was part of the breaking in of the kingdom of God, but not the most important aspect of that inbreaking. The salvation that Jesus brought involves healing the sick. However, until the kingdom comes in its fullness at the resurrection of the dead healing will only be partial.

Healing the sick was not Jesus' primary purpose in the world. Jesus rarely took the initiative in healing. He did not seek out the sick, but healed them as they came along. This demonstrates that healing the sick, exorcising demons, and raising the dead were not the principal purpose of his ministry. The example of the crippled man in John 5:1–9 illustrates this point. Although there were many persons with disabilities in that place, Jesus healed only one. However, Jesus always taught the people. His first priority was proclaiming the gospel and calling people to repentance. The message of Jesus must not be overshadowed by his miracles. Rather, the miracles need to be understood as an indicator that the kingdom of God has arrived (Matt 12:28).

The kingdom of God is first of all about the reign of God over the world and only secondarily about healing of the sick. The miracles were not the ultimate good of the kingdom. Greater than opening the eyes of the blind and unstopping deaf ears, greater than raising the dead to life, was the proclamation of the gospel to the poor. The healings of Jesus were the outward expression of the more important spiritual salvation that he came to bring (compare Luke 17:14, 19). Thus deliverance from physical illness alone is not sufficient without the spiritual deliverance we need. The coming of the kingdom of God involves God's life and power coming into the world. People need relationship with God, not merely his power.

Yet the healings of Jesus were nonetheless an important part of his ministry. Although the miracles were not the primary focus of Jesus' ministry, the healing ministry of Jesus is given a significant amount of space by the Gospel writers. The miracles of Jesus were evidence that the kingdom of God was breaking into the world with power. The kingdom of God had arrived "in him" (Matt 12:28; Luke 11:20). When the disciples of John the Baptist asked if Jesus was really the Messiah, Jesus replied, "The blind receive their sight, the lame walk, the lepers are cleansed, the deaf hear, the dead are raised, and the poor have the good news brought to them" (Matt 11:5). Jesus did more than proclaim the kingdom; he is the kingdom. His miracles are signs of the power of the love of the Father for humanity.

The kingdom that Jesus inaugurated includes healing of the whole person or, in other words, salvation of the whole person. Indeed the person's physical being is given salvation by Jesus Christ. Healing and salvation overlap. When Jesus healed, his healing did not stop at the physical body. When he brought salvation to the soul, it changed the physical aspects of the person. The deliverance of the whole person, which is the salvation we are promised by God, is foreshadowed by the healing miracles of Jesus. So what Jesus did in his ministry was to bring salvation to both soul and body.

But before the *eschaton*—the time of Jesus' return—healing is incomplete. The kingdom of God in the present is not yet the fullness of the future kingdom. Jesus' healings were the first installments of the *eschaton,* when the body will become incorruptible. When the kingdom comes in its fullness, then all who are counted worthy of entering the kingdom (Luke 20:35) will eternally be free from both sickness and death because of the resurrection of the dead. But in the present only some are healed. Although the consummation, or complete fullness, of the kingdom has not yet arrived, it is true that, in the person and ministry of Jesus, God has begun the outworking of salvation for the world.

IS HEALING PHYSICAL OR MORE THAN PHYSICAL?

The healing miracles of Jesus occurred within the context of the coming kingdom of God. The fact that healing of disability is part of the kingdom of God means that it is God's intention to bring complete healing to persons with disabilities when the kingdom of God comes in fullness. But healing is a broad term. It can mean far more than physical cure. On the other hand, physical cure should not be excluded from our understanding of healing.

There is a difference between cure and healing. The idea of healing has become controversial largely because of the post-Enlightenment notion that miraculous healing is not possible. Physical cure is a narrow way to understand healing. Cure involves only the physical dimension, while healing may involve physical cure, psychological relief, spiritual transformation, or indeed other dimensions. Healing as restoration to community and reintegration to society can be possible without the need to believe in the miraculous. Healing can also involve a sense of peace and finding meaning within one's circumstances.

When healing is narrowly defined as cure only, this can have negative consequences for people with disabilities. If we think of healing as physical perfection, people with disabilities can be alienated from the community. On the other hand, in his healing of the sick, Jesus brought about restoration to community for the person with a disability. The lepers were able to go back to worship in the temple; the woman with the issue of blood was able to go back to her community. When barriers are broken down, the person with a disability is affirmed and therefore healed.

Healing is more than cure. But the physical aspect of disability is sometimes ignored in favor of emphasizing social barriers. Many disability writers use a model of disability that sees disability as a social problem. According to the social model of disability, impairment involves a limitation of the person, but disability is the result of social barriers. However, this model will not solve every problem associated with disability. It is true that society does place barriers to access for persons with disabilities, as well as displaying considerable prejudice. It is, nonetheless, not helpful to ignore the real experiences of persons with disabilities. Elimination of barriers and prejudice would not eliminate all aspects of disability. The physical restrictions can still remain a problem even without the social barriers.

Some writers have a very negative attitude towards any kind of physical cure. One objection is that the kingdom of God is welcoming only to the able-bodied. They claim that persons with disabilities are not acceptable as they are, and must be changed to conform to "the norm." According to this idea, Jesus healed people *before* they followed him, implying that he found them unacceptable as they were. They could not follow Jesus while being people with disabilities. However, this way of thinking misreads the Gospel accounts. Jesus did not heal people in order to make them acceptable in the kingdom of God. It is the person of Jesus who makes us acceptable to God. Jesus healed because he had compassion on those who struggled with their disabilities (Matt 14:14, 20:34; Mark 1:41).

In keeping with the realities of physical limitation involved in disability, it is important to notice that the healings of Jesus actually included physical cure. The miracle stories should not be read as metaphors for changing social attitudes or surmounting exclusion. If Jesus' miracles are interpreted as metaphors, then the practical realities of disability are not dealt with in a practical fashion. The metaphorical scenario would imply that the lepers were sent back to their communities still having leprosy, and that Jesus healed the social rifts that excluded the demonized, but they remained mentally ill. Although there is a clear connection between the healing of a sick person and the healing of society, these cannot be fused into one event. To do so is to deny that Jesus took practical measures to give the sick and disabled what was needed. One of the things they needed was physical cure.

An insistence that healing cannot be physical at all reduces healing to less than it can be. Jesus did not merely restore people to community and provide dignity. He also physically cured many people. In fact he did not distinguish between cure and restoration to community, but did both at the same time within his healing ministry. If we are to have a full theological understanding of disability, then we need to have an integrated view of health, salvation, and healing. This means not neglecting physical cure, nor focusing entirely on cure. Healing has spiritual, mental, interpersonal, and social components. In what follows, these different aspects of healing are explored in the ministry of Jesus.

JESUS HEALED MORE THAN BODIES

Jesus healed many people during his ministry. Jesus' healing ministry involved inclusion, presence, acceptance, and genuine compassion. He sought to change social attitudes towards people with disabilities and he challenged cultural structures. Although there are no people with intellectual disabilities mentioned in the Gospel narratives, the way in which Jesus treated children, giving them status, is suggestive of how Jesus would give status to those with intellectual disabilities. Jesus healed the whole person.

Of course Jesus did more than physically cure people. As well as providing physical cure, Jesus had an inclusive attitude towards the outcasts of society. Jesus sided with those who were disparaged by society—those who did not or could not meet society's standards—including the man blind from birth, the paralytic, and other persons with disabilities. He came for those who needed a doctor (Mark 2:17), rather than for those who fitted comfortably within his society. Jesus was unafraid of the consequences of siding with outcasts. Those consequences involved being similarly disparaged. He was maligned, insulted, charged with being the friend of sinners, called a rebel, a heretic, and demon-possessed (Mark 2:16; Luke 5:21, 7:34; John 8:48).

Jesus lived in the midst of persons with disabilities, not apart from them at a distance. Three things can be observed from Jesus' proximity to people with disabilities. First, Jesus was present *with* those who have disabilities. In Luke 7:18–23 the disciples of John the Baptist came to ask Jesus if he was the Messiah. When they arrived Jesus was surrounded by persons with disabilities. He was busy healing their bodies, talking to them, and being with them. For Jesus, persons with disabilities were not objects of fear, but people with whom he chose to be present. Second, in healing the people, Jesus was *doing* the good news; he preached and he acted out the gospel. This good news is that those who are disabled, in both literal and figurative senses, can be healed by the source of all life, Jesus. Third, because Jesus identified with persons with disabilities, he demonstrated a radical acceptance of these people that no one else exhibited.

Jesus did more than feel pity towards the sick; he had compassion on them. Compassion is not the same as pity. Pity tends to be patronizing to those who are pitied. Compassion is better understood as "suffering with another." The New Testament shows that God, in Christ, is compassionate. He did not merely feel sorry for people, but improved their lives through his ministry. The ministry of Jesus demonstrates this compassion in the way he restored the dignity of the sick and people with disabilities (along with other marginalized groups). His compassion thus included both feeling for and acting on behalf of people with disabilities.

Jesus also acted to bring about a change in the attitudes of his society. Mark 3:5 records one of the rare times that Jesus became angry. His anger was directed against the people's attitude towards the man with a disability—he had a withered hand. The people watched to see whether Jesus would heal on the Sabbath. Jesus did not avoid the issue by ignoring the man with a disability. Instead he asked the people, "Is it lawful on the Sabbath to do good or to do harm, to save life or to kill?" The people were concerned with defending a religious dogma, rather than having compassion on the man with a disability. Jesus answered his own question by saying to the man, "Stretch out your hand," and he physically restored the man.

The ministry of Jesus brought about more than a changed life for a few individuals. Jesus challenged the actual structures of his culture. He brought liberation first to the poor. When the disciples of John the Baptist came to ask Jesus if he was the Messiah, "Jesus answered them, 'Go and tell John what you hear and see: the blind receive their sight, the lame walk, the lepers are cleansed, the deaf hear, the dead are raised, and the poor have good news brought to them'" (Matt 11:4–5). It is very significant that the good news was proclaimed to the poor. Paralytics and lepers were indeed poor, with no medical care and no means of support. Also as "sinners" they were socially ostracized. The kingdom of God first affects those who have no rights, the "little ones," and "the least of my brothers" (Matt 18:6, 10, 14; 25:40, 45). These are the ones for whom Jesus changed social structures.

There is no doubt, then, that the ministry of Jesus was significant for people who had physical disabilities. But how did Jesus treat people with intellectual disabilities? It is difficult to find any examples of people with intellectual disabilities in the Gospels. But it is possible to see how Jesus treated those who had inferior status. To attribute intellectual disability to someone is to deny status to that person. "Normal" people are afraid of and disturbed by those who have intellectual disabilities. The treatment of people with intellectual disabilities may be contrasted to how we treat children. It is acceptable to be a child only because children grow into adults and no longer act like children. Yet people with intellectual disabilities do not grow out of acting like children.

In Jesus' day, children had no status in society just as people with intellectual disabilities have no status. The status that Jesus gave to children would therefore have been very surprising to people who heard him. We find the attitude of Jesus recorded in Matt 18:1–4. "At that time the disciples came to Jesus and asked, 'Who is the greatest in the kingdom of heaven?' He called a child, whom he put among them, and said, 'Truly I tell you, unless you change and become like children, you will never enter the kingdom of heaven. Whoever becomes humble like this child is the greatest in the kingdom of heaven.'"

Jesus responded to the disciples' question, "Who is the greatest in the kingdom of heaven?" by using the example of a child. The status of children, rather than some moral characteristic is in view here. A child had a position at the bottom of the social strata, as children were continually subject to the decisions and authority of adults. Yet Jesus accorded a status to children far beyond what his society accorded them. This suggests that Jesus would accord a far greater status to people with intellectual disabilities than is given to them in our culture, and treat them positively.

JESUS IDENTIFIED WITH PEOPLE WITH DISABILITIES

Jesus' healings and his positive attitude towards persons with disabilities are important because the title disabled God could not be given to anyone who failed to show love towards persons with disabilities. However, Jesus' actions and attitudes towards persons with disabilities are not sufficient in themselves to earn him this title. To truly be the disabled God Jesus had to experience disability for himself, and that he did in the cross. But there is another step towards becoming the disabled God. Before becoming disabled himself, he first identified with those who have disabilities. This identification came through living under political oppression, being poor, judging the nations on the basis of how they treat the marginalized, giving of himself in healing, and experiencing the suffering of people with disabilities.

Part of Jesus' identification with persons with disabilities was the fact that he lived within the conditions that are frequent causes of disability worldwide. According to the World Health Organization (WHO), approximately one billion people in the world live with a disability. Possibly up to half of disabilities are preventable. Better nutrition, better medical care, road safety and workplace safety, clean water, and proper sanitation, can all make a difference to the number of disabilities. Poverty can both increase the likelihood of disability and exacerbate the difficulties of having a disability. Two out of three people with disabilities live in developing countries. Political instability and war can result in increased poverty and lack of social welfare. These situations make poor health more likely.

Palestine at the time of Jesus' birth was a politically oppressed nation. Palestine had been oppressed by the Romans for hundreds of years. They had a godless king in Herod the Great and were occupied by foreign armies, as well as being subject to high taxation levied by those foreign rulers. In this society there was no economic security; there was a frequent need to look for work and consequently money would often be in short supply. Into this politically oppressed nation Jesus was born poor. After his birth Jesus was laid in a manger. This was a humble beginning to a life of poverty. Jesus became poor and gave over everything to free those who are poor (2 Cor 8:9). He also lived with powerlessness. Jesus did not act to rescue himself from the hunger that he experienced when he fasted in the desert (Matt 4:2). In the same way he refused to come down from the cross (Matt 27:40).

Another way in which Jesus expressed his identification with persons with disabilities is in the parable of the sheep and the goats (Matt 25:31–46). The nations will be judged according to how they act towards the hungry, the thirsty, the naked, the sick, and those in prison. When those at the judgment ask when they fed a hungry Jesus or clothed his nakedness, "the king will answer them, 'Truly I tell you, just as you did it to one of the least of these who are members of my family, you did it to me'" (Matt 25:40). This verse suggests that God is hidden in the other, in our neighbor who is in need. God is present in the weak and marginalized. Jesus here characterizes faithfulness towards his person in terms of compassionate actions. The mystery revealed in this parable is that the presence of God is found in those whose value appears to be little.

Jesus identified with the sick he healed in that every healing took place at some expense to himself. Each healing brought some harm to Jesus. The woman with the issue of blood (Mark

5:30) caused power to go out from Jesus. When Jesus healed on the Sabbath he consistently came into conflict. After healing the leper (Mark 1:41), Jesus became isolated while the leper was free to re-enter society. In showing compassion for a grieving woman (Luke 7:13) or for blind men (Matt 20:34), Jesus demonstrated his empathy. But his compassion went further than this. When Jesus cried tears with Lazarus' sisters (John 11:35), he actually entered into their experience of loss and grief and thereby bore it.

Jesus' power to heal the sick came through his suffering. Jesus did not heal the sick by means of magic, but by means of faith. The answer to how Jesus was able to heal lies in the passage that Matt 8:17 quotes from Isa 53:4, "He took our infirmities and bore our diseases." Jesus healed the sick by bearing their diseases; he took the sicknesses and disabilities upon himself. Jesus' healing of the sick and people with disabilities pointed to the cross. The life of Jesus was a path of suffering that led from his lowly birth in obscure Bethlehem to his humiliating and painful death on Golgotha. On this path Jesus healed the sick, loved sinners, integrated the outcasts, and cast out demons. It is not the deity of Jesus Christ, then, that gave him the power to heal the sick, but rather his willingness to suffer and die for humanity.

His identification with people who were sick and marginalized involved suffering on the part of Jesus, but suffering was not the end point of Jesus' ministry. He was raised from the dead and his miracles point us toward that fact. There are two words used in the New Testament for resurrection, *anistēmi* and *egeirō*. The way in which *egeirō* is used in the New Testament is unique because it is used when speaking of raising up the sick. Since the word is also is used of Jesus' resurrection, this is a sign that healings are intended to show us something about the resurrection in advance. Jesus' healing miracles herald the new condition of humanity in which "death will be no more; mourning and crying and pain will be no more, for the first things have passed away" (Rev 21:4).

CONCLUSION

Jesus' ministry to persons with disabilities was a very positive one. He healed many people as he ushered in the kingdom of God. Thus his healings and the salvation he offered were connected with one another. The fullness of the kingdom has not yet arrived, but it will bring the redemption of the body. When Jesus healed persons with disabilities, this healing was multifaceted. It included physical cure, reconciliation of relationships, reintegration into community, compassion, inclusion, and transformation of society. Jesus also accorded status to those without status, suggesting that he would have valued people with intellectual disabilities. Jesus began to identify with persons with disabilities even in his life, experiencing physical oppression and poverty, bearing the consequences of healing people, and having compassion on them.

At this point it is fair to say that Jesus had earned the title God of the disabled, but he had not yet earned the title the disabled God. For Jesus to be given the title the disabled God requires a number of things: he must be fully God and fully human; he must have a positive relationship with persons with disabilities; and he must experience disability himself. So far chapter 1 has argued his status as the God-man and chapter 2 has argued that Jesus spent a large amount of time with persons with disabilities and met their needs in multifaceted ways. The next chapter will examine the cross of Christ and his experience of disability in his person.

3

The Cross

INTRODUCTION

CHRIST FREELY EMPTIED HIMSELF in the incarnation and entered into the world in which disability is common. During his ministry Jesus healed many persons with disabilities as part of ushering in the kingdom of God. In both his free acceptance of mortality and in his positive treatment of persons with disabilities, Jesus identified with persons with disabilities. Thus far Jesus could rightly be called the God of the disabled. But he cannot be called the disabled God unless he has experienced disability himself. This he did when on the cross. He went to the cross, not by happenstance, but by intention; he freely chose to allow others to crucify him in order to save humanity from sin. On the cross Jesus experienced what it is to be a person with disabilities—physically, socially, and emotionally. Thus on the cross Jesus truly became the disabled God. There are several results of this disabling experience on the cross: it changed the way in which the Trinity understands disability; it provides a theodicy; ability is now found in weakness; and finally there are implications for persons with disabilities.

DIVINE FREEDOM AND THE INTENTIONALITY OF THE CROSS

God is free to become other than himself and hence was free to become incarnate. But the freedom of God is not absolute. God is free to choose actions consistent with his own character. And the Son of God was free to choose only actions that were in keeping with his sonship and his mission given by the Father. Jesus desires only obedience to his Father. Jesus emptied himself and humbled himself even to death on a cross (Phil 2:7–8), and this humiliation was no chance occurrence. Jesus chose this humiliation freely because he is the obedient Son. And yet there can be no other choice if he is to be consistent with himself. If he were to choose to not go to the cross, then he would no longer be the obedient Son and hence no longer himself. So his choice was free and yet necessitated by who he is.

It is vital to understand that the death of Jesus on the cross was no accident of history, but rather a part of the divine plan for the salvation of the human race. God the Father was the hidden initiator behind the cross. It was the self-giving love of God (Rom 5:8) for humanity that motivated the Father to send the Son to the cross. It was the willing obedience of the Son, who submits to the will of the Father (Gal 1:4), that brought about the salvation of humanity. Jesus did not bend the Father's will nor was the resurrection a response of pity towards the martyred Jesus by the Father. All these events were planned in advance by the Father in order to accomplish his loving purposes for the human race.

The Scriptures, both Old and New Testaments, assert the inevitability of the cross. "Christ died for our sins in accordance with the Scriptures" (1 Cor 15:3). The death of Jesus was a divine certainty; it happened according to God's clear plan. The fact that Jesus predicted his own death, as the Gospels record, points to the same inevitability. He accepted his own death as part of his mission. The Synoptic Gospels (Matthew, Mark, and Luke) contain three main predictions of Jesus' passion (Mark 8:31; 9:31; 10:33–34; plus parallel passages). These passion predictions in the mouth of Jesus imply that Jesus was not surprised by events in Jerusalem, by his suffering and his death.

Knowing that suffering, rejection, and death awaited him there, Jesus deliberately went to Jerusalem. Luke 9:51 records, "When the days drew near for him to be taken up, he set his face to go to Jerusalem." Several New Testament passages record Jesus' willingness to die for humanity (e.g., John 10:15). His decision to go to Jerusalem was deliberate despite the inescapability of his death. Jesus was not simply in the wrong place at the wrong time. His disciples did not convince him to make the journey to Jerusalem. Jesus made a deliberate and free decision to go to his death in Jerusalem because he understood this action to be the climax of his divinely appointed mission.

Jesus' death was the continuation of his life, which he lived in the service of others. Jesus might have prevented his death by backing away from his ministry and message, but he did not. His words and his actions provoked his opponents into bringing about his death. He lived for others and he died for others, demonstrating his great love for humanity. Medieval theologian Bernard of Clairvaux (died 1153) wrote about the compassion of Jesus, "Such was the example shown by our Savior, who desired to suffer himself in order that he might learn how to show mercy."[1]

Jesus' deliberate decision to endure the cross means that he made a deliberate decision to allow himself to become disabled. In this sense he was not a hapless victim in his disablement, as so many people are, but he was a victim nonetheless. To be the disabled God requires that there was willingness to take on disability. Jesus did not shy away from the consequences of the life he intended to live. A life lived for the weak, the marginalized, and the disabled, culminated in the Son of God becoming weak, marginalized, and disabled. In becoming the disabled God upon the cross, Jesus demonstrated the heart of the Father to those who suffer disability.

---

1. Bernard of Clairvaux. *Treatise on the Degrees of Humility and Pride*, 1121.

JESUS TOOK ON DISABILITY ON THE CROSS

His deliberate choice to go to the cross meant that Jesus actually experienced physical disability and weakness there. In his passion he became blind for a time and severely weakened. His death included the experience of paralysis, physical pain, blood loss, and being without a voice. Although it is impossible to spell out precise features of every disease and disability in the experience of Jesus, it is true to say that on the cross Jesus identified with all those who have a physical disability. Therefore, the title disabled God can be applied literally to Jesus in his passion.

To understand the disabling of Jesus on the cross it is instructive to have a general understanding of crucifixion. There was a great deal of variability in the form of the execution because the soldiers were permitted to give full vent to their own sadism, but a "typical" procedure can be described. Before the crucifixion the victim was flogged and often expected to carry the crossbeam to the site of the crucifixion. Then the person was nailed to the crossbeam, and, when vertical, the person's weight would be supported by a small piece of wood. The torture that resulted continued for a long time. First-century Roman philosopher Seneca described the agony of the cross:

> Can anyone be found who would prefer wasting away in pain, dying limb by limb, or letting out his life drop by drop, rather than expiring once for all? Can any man be found willing to be fastened to the accursed tree, longing sickly, already deformed, swelling with ugly tumors on chest and shoulders, and drawing the breath of life amid long-drawn-out agony? I think he would have many excuses for dying even before mounting the cross![2]

The cross is inherently disabling. Crucifixion would have made it almost impossible to function as a human being on any significant level because of the extreme and unrelenting pain. Being pinned to a cross meant that Jesus was unable to move his limbs, was barely able to breathe, and could do none of the most

2. Seneca, Lucius Annaeus. *Moral Epistles*, CI, circa 65.

basic human activities, such as eating or drinking, without the assistance of sadistic soldiers. There is very little about this experience that would not be called disabling.

What follows is a description of some of the specific disabilities that Jesus experienced on the cross. As Jesus went through his passion he took on many of the disabilities that he had healed during his ministry. In this way Jesus fully identified with persons with disabilities by experiencing what they experience.

Jesus identified with blind people during his passion. Whenever Jesus came across people who were blind he restored their sight; he did not merely offer acceptance and inclusion. Jesus spoke of healing the blind as central to his ministry (Luke 4:18). Yet it was following Jesus' arrest that he identified most fully with blind people. Mark 14:65 records, "Some began to spit on him, to blindfold him, and to strike him, saying to him 'Prophesy!' The guards also took him over and beat him." Because of this humiliation and ridicule, which took place when he was without power to tell who was hitting him (Luke 22:64), Jesus knows what it is to experience the obstacles and powerlessness of blindness.

The next disabling event was severe weakness, most likely brought about by the flogging, which meant Jesus was unable to carry his own cross to Golgotha. "They compelled a passer-by, who was coming in from the country, to carry his cross; it was Simon of Cyrene, the father of Alexander and Rufus" (Mark 15:21). Perhaps the community to which Mark wrote was keen to remember the miracles of Jesus and to forget about the cross. Mark wanted them to see that it is the suffering and weak Jesus who calls people to follow him and suffer with him. The now risen Jesus is the same person who was too weak to carry his own cross.

Jesus suffered in his passion in a way that parallels the bleeding woman described in Mark 5:25–34. When Jesus met this socially ostracized woman, she was healed by touching his garment. It is likely that Mark intended to use this example to show the reader the parallels to the passion story via the use of particular words. The woman suffered at the hands of doctors and Jesus also suffered (Mark 5:26; 8:31; 9:12). The blood of the woman is analogous to that of Jesus. Mark uses the word "body" only in this story and the story of the passion. "Scourge" is another link between the two events. The woman's illness is called a scourge (noun; Mark 5:29), and scourge (verb; Mark 10:34) is used in regard to what Jesus endured.

Jesus went to his death without a voice to be heard. In his ministry Jesus healed several people who were unable to speak (e.g., Matt 9:33; 12:22; 15:30). In his death he became the mute lamb mentioned in the servant song of Isaiah (52:13—53:12). "Like a lamb that is led to the slaughter, and like a sheep that before its shearers is silent [mute], so he did not open his mouth" (Isa 53:7). This passage describes the inability of the servant, yet paradoxically this accomplishes the will of Yahweh. Here mute means both inability (compare Ps 39:9) and obedience (compare Ps 38:13–15), and in both the power of God is enigmatically brought to completion. In this way he identified with those who have no voice, either literally or metaphorically.

Jesus bore in his body many of the disabling conditions of which he had healed people during his ministry, including paralysis. There can be no greater weakness than that which results from being nailed to a cross, experiencing extreme pain on the way to death. When Jesus was nailed to the cross he had no control over his body. He was not in control of his bodily functions. He was at the mercy of others, who chose not to care for him in his weakness, but rather to mock him. His weakness was thus extreme.

Although it might be possible to continue to list disabilities that Jesus experienced on the cross, I prefer to take a different approach. The Gospel writers do not seem interested in going into depth in their descriptions of the crucifixion. Mark 15:24 states baldly, "and they crucified him." This lack of detail means that the experience of Jesus can be applicable to all persons with disabilities in the present since he bore disabilities of many kinds.

There is no doubt that being nailed to a cross would have caused Jesus to lose control over his body, but there is much that cannot be said about Jesus' experience of disability on the cross. It is not possible to state categorically that Jesus experienced the symptoms of multiple sclerosis, for example, because there is simply not enough detail to draw on. The disabling of Jesus must be thought of in more general terms. In this way people with disabilities can see that on the cross Jesus had much in common with them, even though a particular person's disability may not be identifiable in the passion narrative. It was his vulnerable state that enabled him to identify with all those who are helpless and vulnerable, all those who are weak and ignored, all those who are dismissed as less than human because of their disability.

In addition to his physical disablement, in dying the death of a helpless man, Jesus also seems to have lost the messianic anointing by which he healed the sick during his ministry. Matthew's passion story shows a Jesus who had given up his power and authority. Instead of looking like the mighty Son of God, Jesus became god-forsaken. John's Gospel takes up this idea in a different fashion. In John's account Jesus said, "I am thirsty" (John 19:28), pointing to the irony that the person who once offered the water of life to others then needed to ask for a drink. On the cross all power to heal the sick and bring about the kingdom of God seemed lost. Indeed the opposite of kingdom power was present. God was, at best, no longer actively present, or, at worst, apparently not present at all. Thus the death of Jesus stood in sharp contrast with his life.

INTELLECTUAL DISABILITY AND THE CROSS

Not only did Jesus identify with persons with physical disabilities, but he also identified with persons with intellectual disabilities. Jesus is the disabled God in terms of intellectual disability as well as physical disability. Fourth-century church father Gregory of Nazianzus wisely observed, "What is unassumed is unhealed." Consequently, Jesus needed to identify with persons with intellectual disability so that he would bring healing to them. While it is possible to see that Jesus experienced physical disability on the cross, it is more difficult to see how Jesus identified with persons with intellectual disabilities in his passion. There is no evidence to suggest that Jesus had an intellectual disability on the cross. However, it is not necessary for Jesus to have an intellectual disability for him to identify with those who do. The most fundamental aspect of intellectual disability is not a particular IQ or medical criterion, but the fact that people with intellectual disabilities are disadvantaged because of difference. It is the disadvantage that Jesus needed to experience in order to identify with those who have an intellectual disability.

Jesus identified with persons with intellectual disabilities through his experiences of loneliness, poverty, shame, and stigma in his passion. Loneliness, poverty, shame, and stigma do not exclusively apply to people with intellectual disabilities. However, people with intellectual disabilities probably experience the above in greater degree than others, even more so than those with physical disabilities. To demonstrate Jesus' identification with persons with intellectual disabilities we first need to understand the lives of those with intellectual disability. Here I will explore different aspects of those lives and show the parallels between those experiences and the experience of Jesus on the cross.

People with intellectual disabilities are regularly excluded and are consequently very lonely. They are frequently excluded from participating in groups of "normal" people. To be excluded is dehumanizing and painful to the excluded person. Exclusion diminishes the person and implies that the excluded person is undeserving of being part of human interaction. Jean Vanier is the founder of L'Arche communities, where people with intellectual disabilities live side by side with people of normal intelligence. He is well placed to comment on the exclusion of people with intellectual disabilities. He observes, "I have come to the conclusion that those with intellectual disabilities are among the most oppressed and excluded people in the world. Even their own parents are frequently ashamed to have given birth to a child 'like that.'"[3]

Jesus experienced the extremes of loneliness and exclusion on the cross. After many hours on the cross, Jesus cried out, "'*Eloi, Eloi, lema sabachthani?*' which means, 'My God, my God, why have you forsaken me?'" (Mark 15:34b). When Jesus cried out he

3. Vanier, Jean. *Becoming Human*. New York, NY: Paulist, 1998, 72.

felt completely forsaken by both human beings and by God. All the people in Jesus' life—his family and country-people, the king and the religious leaders, his chosen disciples, and all the people of Jerusalem—had left him alone to die a despised death inflicted by the enemy Romans. At that moment it was as if he did not experience the fellowship of God either, even though he had always experienced it up to that point. What an incredibly lonely time, a time when Jesus would have most needed someone and yet there was no one.

Poverty is so often an unwanted adjunct to having a disability. Many persons with disabilities are amongst the world's poorest people. People with intellectual impairments are less likely to complete school and have the lowest rates of employment. They are three or four times less likely to be employed than are other people with disabilities. Lack of employment generally results in poverty, and the kinds of employment open to people with intellectual disabilities are not highly paid. Therefore, even those who are employed may experience poverty. They also suffer from problems that accompany poverty—poor housing, poor medical treatment, and poor opportunities.

Like so many persons with disabilities, Jesus endured extreme poverty on the cross. Crucifixion was the punishment for slaves, and those slaves had to endure the capriciousness of their masters in life. It was standard practice for the victim to be crucified naked. Therefore, it is possible to see that Jesus suffered the death of the lowest rank in society. On the cross he did not even have the basic necessity of clothing to cover him. He had nothing at all of his own in his death, not even his dignity. Thus he identified with the world's poor in his passion.

In addition to loneliness and poverty there is a distinct sense of stigma and shame attached to being disabled. In many, if not most, periods in history, people with disabilities have been perceived as less than human. While the degree of stigma varies, the experience of being stigmatized is common to all persons with disabilities. Throughout the world, most persons with disabilities experience stigmatization resulting in discrimination, derision, condescension, and exclusion. This particularly applies to people with intellectual disabilities because being different is enough to stigmatize them. There is a strong sense of blame attached to disability. Even with a scientific world-view many people still secretly believe that persons with disabilities and their families are in some way to blame for that disability.

Jesus identified with those who experience shame and stigma in that crucifixion was the most shameful death in the ancient world. Crucifixion was a death meant for criminals. First-century Jewish author Josephus called it "the most wretched of deaths."[4] The executioners intentionally subjected the victim to extreme humiliation. So despised was the act of crucifixion, and the fate of the criminal assigned such a punishment, that mention was hardly made of crucifixion in ancient inscriptions. First-century-BC Roman philosopher Cicero expresses the horror of even the mention of the word:

> But the executioner, the veiling of the head and the very word 'cross' should be far removed not only from the person of a Roman citizen but from his thoughts, his eyes, and his ears. For it is not only the actual occurrence of these things or the endurance of them, but liability to them, the expectation, indeed the very mention of them, that is unworthy of a Roman citizen and a free man.[5]

Sadly, religious vilification is a common experience for people with intellectual disabilities, even in the Christian church. Some churches have barred people with physical and intellectual disabilities from being ordained. The attitude that underlies this decision may spring from the belief that people who are not physically whole cannot represent the perfect man, Jesus. This attitude towards persons with disabilities extends further than exclusion from ordination. Many persons with disabilities have been denied a meaningful place in their churches because of those disabilities. One researcher reports the case of a twenty-year-old man with

4. Josephus, Flavius. *The Jewish War,* 7.203, circa 75.
5. Cicero, Marcus Tillius. *For Rabirius on a Charge of Treason,* 5.16, 63 BC.

cerebral palsy, who was not permitted to sing in the choir because the pastor thought he was strange.

There were religious dimensions to the shame of the cross that gave Jesus something further in common with people with intellectual disabilities. The Jews of Jesus' time looked at crucifixion through the lens of Deut 21:23, "anyone hung on a tree is under God's curse." The religious aspects of the shame of crucifixion added to the general denigration of the victim in the common mindset. Jesus was considered a blasphemer by the religious leaders. The manner of his death seemed to emphasize this view; he was put to death outside the holy city of Jerusalem (Heb 13:12) like one rejected and condemned.

It is difficult to talk about Jesus having an intellectual disability on the cross. To say that Jesus identified with people with intellectual disabilities by experiencing cognitive impairment would be to go beyond what the Gospel accounts tell of his death. However, Jesus did identify with persons with intellectual disabilities in his experience of loneliness, poverty, shame and stigma, and religious vilification as he was crucified. Jesus is truly the disabled God because he was physically disabled on the cross and he identified with persons with intellectual disabilities in the negative experiences that they commonly face.

CONSEQUENCES OF THE DISABLED GOD

Having reached the conclusion that Jesus is truly the disabled God—because of his identification with persons with disabilities on the cross—the question must be asked: so what? What difference does it make that Jesus is the disabled God? The answer has two dimensions: it makes a difference to God himself, and it makes a difference to people with disabilities. For God, the experience of Jesus on the cross has changed the way in which God understands disability. Before the cross, God did not know what it was like to experience human disability. On the human side, the cross provides a theodicy (a defense of God's goodness in the face of suffering), a new view of weakness, and changes for people with disabilities. I begin with the effect of the cross on the Trinity.

THE CROSS AND THE TRINITY

What does Jesus' experience of disability on the cross mean for the Godhead? Both Jesus and the Father experienced the cross, but in different ways. The Father delivered up the Son to death. "He who did not withhold his own Son, but gave him up for all of us, will he not with him also give us everything else?" (Rom 8:32). Jesus' death involved all that being delivered up means for sinful humanity. God delivers up sinners to their own sinfulness (Rom 1:24, 26, 28), and this handing over into godlessness is the punishment for their abandonment of God. God's solution to the godforsakenness of the godless is the godforsakenness of the Son on the cross.

But it is not merely that the Son was delivered up to suffering and death, this suffering was a suffering within the Trinity. As the Son died in godforsakenness on the cross, the Father also suffered in his delivering up of the Son. The Father's suffering was different to the Son's. For Jesus, the suffering was something physical. For the Father, the suffering was pain that came from watching his Son die. The Father experienced grief and sorrow as the Son died. Yet in this separation of Father and Son there was a profound unity of purpose. The Son also gave himself up, according to Gal 2:20b— "the Son of God, who loved me and gave himself for me." The will of the Son was fully in accord with the will of the Father in the cross and, as such, there was both fellowship in their separation and separation in their fellowship.

In the cross were desolation, godforsakenness, and even death, eternal condemnation, infinite emptiness, and non-being. Because Jesus has experienced these things, so has God. This profoundly negative experience for Jesus is the basis for our positive experience of God, of salvation, joy, and sharing in the divine life. The death of Jesus has become part of "the history of God," that is, the experience of God, both Father and Son. As a result, all human history is incorporated into this history of God and human beings "in Christ" are able to participate in God's future, which involves salvation, joy, and life.

The eternal God did not merely limit himself, but became disabled, weak, powerless, and subject to death like mortal humanity. When Jesus became disabled on the cross, this had an effect on the Trinity. The Father did not become disabled because human disability requires becoming a human being, but the Father did experience suffering because of Jesus' weakness, loneliness, abandonment, and shame. He suffered while the Son was unable. He suffered while the Son was vilified. His suffering included grief, sorrow, and emotional pain over his Son's separation and physical suffering. These aspects of disability have become part of the history of God. Because he was disabled, disability will be fully healed by Jesus. But God himself is not disabled, nor can the Father experience human disability directly. God knows the reality of persons with disabilities only because he has experienced this reality in the disabling of Jesus on the cross. Jesus has taken this experience into God by virtue of his unique status as the God-man.

The fact that God, in Jesus Christ, has become the disabled God on the cross does not imply that God is not omnipotent. For God "all things are possible" (Matt 19:26). But the disabled God demonstrates that God is *free to be weak*. In Christ, God has freely chosen to suffer in the way that human beings suffer. This does not mean that God is not omnipotent, but only that, in his omnipotence, he is free to empty himself and become impotent for the sake of love. He is strong enough to allow himself to be weak.

By his submission to death on the cross, Christ has taken death and, as a consequence, disability into God himself. This action brought about a change in the Trinity in that now death and disability have become part of the history of God. Yet the result of Jesus' humiliation is not the eternalizing of disability within God, but rather the extinguishing of death and disability. This is possible because Jesus is uniquely both God and human being simultaneously. Disability does not add to God, but Jesus' taking on of disability has added to our understanding of God's omnipotence because of his freedom to make himself impotent in the cross.

THEODICY

The cross has had an effect on God, but it also has an effect on humans. It is difficult to ignore the fact that the world is not perfect and that suffering occurs in it. Some people experience suffering through their physical and intellectual disabilities. Much of that suffering is the result of human actions and discrimination. But some of the difficulties are inherent to the impairment itself. Wherever the difficulties arise from, the question is often asked: how can God allow this to happen? The answer to this is found in the cross.

The cross is the ultimate theodicy; it is the ultimate answer to what God is doing about suffering. When Job was afflicted with suffering he voiced a cry of protest to God that may be a cry for all the afflicted. "Do you have eyes of flesh? Do you see as humans see?" (Job 10:4). How far can God go in identifying with those who suffer? It is not possible to give a cogent reply to Job's question because there is no reason why suffering must be a good within a universe created by a God of love. If such an answer were to be formulated, it would serve only to make suffering acceptable, even something to celebrate, as part of God's good creation. The only possible way of making Job's experience meaningful is the answer given by the crucified one. The answer that Jesus gives is not simply as the man who suffered and died to redeem humanity from sin, because that suffering had a purpose. But Job's suffering was purposeless and meaningless. The word that gives meaning to Job's experience comes from Jesus the God-man, who died as the one who was godforsaken in his pain. He is the God who knows the suffering of Job.

The cross is a surprising theodicy. God fails to "do something" about suffering in the way that human beings want him to. What is totally surprising is that God participates in suffering. Love is never love without solidarity with the beloved. God's solidarity with humankind is demonstrated by the incarnation, in which God was willing to become a victim. Ultimately the cross demonstrates that God not only wages war against human suffering, but he does this in solidarity with suffering humanity by becoming a suffering man. The suffering of Jesus introduces a third option in dealing with suffering. Instead of accepting suffering as noble or removing suffering from without, Jesus has borne it. If God is silent in the face of suffering, it is because he has also suffered in order to bring all suffering to an end.

Jesus' experience of disability on the cross means that God's love for persons with disabilities has been demonstrated in a trustworthy way. The cross shows the true depth of God's love for humanity. This love cannot be understood from an appreciation of creation. It can *only* be known through the cross of Christ. Entering into the pain of history discloses a God whose love is wholly credible. This brokenness of God permits the church to speak credibly to those who are suffering because the church was formed through the torment, desecration, and distortion of Christ's body.

Persons with disabilities need not question the love of God nor need they question why disability has become part of their experience. God has not ignored the fact of disability in the world, but has freely submitted himself to all that disability entails, in solidarity with those who suffer because of their disabilities. Jesus has not called disability good or stood outside and temporarily removed it, but rather he has healed it from the inside by bearing it (although the final healing will not happen until Jesus returns). This makes the disabled God a God of credible love for persons with disabilities, and enables the church to minister to persons with disabilities because her God is the disabled God.

ABILITY IN WEAKNESS

Now let us consider the way in which the cross transforms ideas of strength and weakness. One significant aspect of the disabled God is his weakness on the cross in contrast to the traditional philosophical ideal of an omnipotent God. This power in weakness must change any understanding of disability amongst the people of God.

The powerlessness and weakness of Jesus on the cross has brought about a transformation of reality. No longer can we think of God as omnipotent according to the philosophical understanding that we may have had before. We might imagine that God is all powerful according to our ideas of human power extended to greater heights. But in fact God's power is not what we would expect. It is in the cross that God demonstrates his power. "For the message about the cross is foolishness to those who are perishing, but to us who are being saved it is the power of God" (1 Cor 1:18). "God's weakness is stronger than human strength" (1 Cor 1:25). Because God's power is made perfect in weakness (2 Cor 12:9), it is necessary to experience weakness, as Jesus did in the cross, in order to know the power of God.

We may consider this idea further in relation to disability by looking at the Greek word *astheneia*. This is usually translated as "weakness," but it may be translated as "inability." If we use this translation, then in 2 Cor 12:5–10 Paul glories in his inabilities because God has spoken directly to him saying, "My power is made complete in inability." Thus Paul can conclude, "When I lack ability then I am able." This seeming paradox of a God who is all powerful, yet whose power is completed in inability, is explained by the cross of Christ. For Paul, the cross stands at the center (1 Cor 1:23; 2:2; Gal 6:14). The fact that the Messiah was crucified is inherently contradictory for both Jew and Gentile. Yet it was in the cross that God perfectly manifested his power and love through the complete inability of Jesus Christ.

Paul believes that his lack of ability is evidence that that Christ's power rests on him (2 Cor 12:9b). The word Paul uses here for "rest," *episkēnoō*, is used only once in the New Testament. It evokes the idea of a tent like that of the Old Testament tabernacle. This tabernacle was the place where sacrifice took place, according to the book of Leviticus. In the levitical tradition, a priest with inabilities was excluded from the tabernacle and from offering sacrifice (Lev 21:16–23). Yet Paul has tipped this tradition on its head as he says God's power is made complete in weakness and Christ's power finds its place to dwell in inability.

The result of this new paradigm of power in weakness is a different view of those who are weak and needy. The cross of Christ brings about a new understanding of being human. Dependence, not independence, is the path to a full life; need is no longer a bane, for now it opens the door to life and blessing. People who are weak have been given gifts that the church cannot do without. "The members of the body that seem to be weaker are indispensable" (1 Cor 12:22). What we think about weakness is completely upturned by the cross.

The cross changes the meaning of disability because it changes the meaning of weakness. This radically different perspective on disability needs to reshape the way Christians think about disability and those who live with disability. It must also reshape the way people with disabilities think about themselves.

THE EFFECT OF THE DISABLED GOD ON PERSONS WITH DISABILITIES

The disabled God can have an effect on people with disabilities themselves. Jesus the disabled God gives dignity to people with disabilities. His suffering means that those who suffer can cry out to God in their pain. People with disabilities are given new status because the disabled God has transformed all notions of status. Suffering is no longer meaningless, but something that is meaningfully done in Christ. And the cross provides hope because Jesus has conquered death.

Many people with disabilities prefer not to equate disability with suffering. They want to be acknowledged as people who live ordinary lives as best they can. Yet there is an element of physical and sometimes mental suffering involved in having a disability, regardless of whether society provides access and a positive place for people who are impaired. Suffering also often results from the attitudes of others towards the person with the disability. Ill-treatment and wrong attitudes are not justifiable. But since human beings will never be perfected by political correctness, this suffering may well not go away. The cross of Jesus is the place where God shared that suffering.

The cross bestows dignity and meaning to those who experience disability because God has entered into that experience. It is a sad fact that those who are physically and mentally unimpaired often deny that people who suffer are genuine persons because this effectively helps us to keep our distance from suffering. In contrast to this, by participating in human suffering on the cross, Jesus sanctified suffering and thus afforded dignity to even the most miserable facets of human experience. God's wretchedness in the cross can give meaning to the believer in the present difficulties and disruptions of life, not just in the future.

The cross gives those who are suffering a precedent for crying out to God in their pain. Hurt and anger that result from pain do not need to be suppressed because Jesus gave vent to his feelings of grief and desolation on the cross (Mark 15:34). This is true whether it is physical, mental, or emotional pain, whether it is caused by another person or not. If God was present in the seeming abandonment of Jesus on the cross, then God is present for the believer even when no consciousness of that presence exists. The cross offers no rationales for suffering, but rather it confers the power to endure in hope because Jesus has gone before by calling out to God, even in his abandonment.

The cross also transforms existing ideas of social status and importance. In 1 Cor 1:18—2:5 Paul discusses wisdom and strength in light of the cross. It is not that the foolish and weak Corinthian Christians were made strong and wise. Their human capabilities remained the same, but the gospel brings liberation from the old outlook that determines social status. Many of the Corinthians were poor, uneducated, and without political suffrage (1:26); their social status was low. Yet because these people were the elect of God, they were able to view themselves in a different light; they were no longer inferior to those who seem to be wise and strong. "God chose what is low and despised in the world, things that are not, to reduce to nothing things that are" (1:28). The cross tips upside-down all notions of wisdom and power, weakness and strength.

Consequently, the cross gives a new status within the church to persons with disabilities. This is important because many people falsely believe that persons with disabilities cannot represent Jesus, who was perfect. But Jesus was not perfect in the sense of physical perfection. During his passion he was scourged to the point of being unable to carry his own cross. Whatever strength and ability he had left was removed by the act of crucifixion, which left Jesus physically disabled as well as humiliated. The idea that persons with disabilities cannot represent Jesus must be disputed in the light of the disabled God. Having a physical disability should not prevent ordination or participation in ministry.

Just as death is overcome by the death of Jesus, so too is healing effected by the cross, and will be brought to completion in the resurrection of the dead. Medieval mysticism understood something of the healing afforded by the wounds of Jesus. Mysticism viewed the cross of Christ differently to the more normative view of the cross as reconciling sacrifice. It involved meditation on the sufferings of Christ and his nearness to those who suffer. Because of his pain and anguish on the cross, Jesus is a particular comfort to those who are poor, sick, or deeply hurt, while no one else can be of any help. The mystics correctly understood that our suffering is overcome by Jesus' suffering and our wounds healed by his.

There is comfort found in the wounded Christ. Christ is in no way separate from his people. Jesus has one body, of which he is the head, and the people in the church are his members. Jesus did not suffer merely in the past, but he continues to suffer in the present because his body, the church, suffers (Acts 9:4). The pain that his church feels is borne by him; it is his pain. Knowing that Christ experienced human misery changes us psychologically. There is real comfort in this fact.

Because of the cross, suffering is transformed from something that is meaningless and must be simply endured alone to something that is done in Christ. Jesus has purified suffering. Suffering is no longer part of the meaninglessness of existence, or the result of past personal sins, or even the outcome of incurring God's wrath. Those who are in Christ experience suffering completely differently to those who are not. This is because Christ is God's response to suffering and Christians suffer as a part of that response. Therefore, Christians do not suffer alone, but in communion with Jesus. Sharing the suffering of Jesus is part of sharing in the purposes of God in the world.

On the cross, Jesus has brought about hope for all people by conquering death. This hope springs from the fact that Jesus has gone through the experience of suffering and death and is now raised from the dead. He has died, but can never die again; he has suffered and has overcome suffering; he has experienced fear, but is forever free from fear. The crucified one is the basis of God's new creation, in which death is abolished by life and suffering is brought to an end. The emptiness and meaninglessness of death has been taken into God by Jesus and thus people can now live in the hope of the new creation. The new creation will come to completion in the resurrection of the dead.

CONCLUSION

The cross is the place in which Jesus became the disabled God in experience. Prior to this event it was possible to call Jesus the God of the disabled because he willingly emptied himself and entered into the human experience, with the chance of becoming disabled. In his ministry, Jesus spent time with persons with disabilities and brought them healing in all its facets: physical, emotional, spiritual, and relational. Yet in none of this could Jesus truly be called the disabled God because he had not experienced what it was to be a person with a disability.

The cross is the rightful center for understanding the disabled God. It is on the cross that Jesus experienced disability and all that it entails—incapacity, inability, physical pain, mental suffering, weakness, poverty, shame, and abandonment. Although Jesus did not become intellectually disabled, he did experience the extreme discrimination, loneliness, and loss of personhood that people with intellectual disabilities face regularly. Because of these experiences, it is possible to give Jesus the title of the disabled God in every sense. Jesus deliberately went towards the cross in accord with the will of the Father. He has become the disabled God by intention not by accident. Because of this, Jesus can speak powerfully to persons with disabilities as one who has entered into their reality.

The implications of the disabled God are many. For the Trinity there has been a change in that disability has been taken into the history of God. God has not become impotent, but he freely chose to empty himself of his omnipotence in the cross. The result is that disability has been borne to extinction in God. That Jesus took on disability has also served to justify God in the face of disability; God is now credibly a God of love for persons with disabilities. Power and weakness have been transformed; weakness is now the place of God's presence. Finally, the disabled God has given new dignity, status, healing, comfort, and hope to persons with disabilities.

The story of the disabled God does not, indeed cannot, end with the cross. Jesus rose from the dead immortal and is seated at God's right hand. Without his resurrection from the dead the cross is nothing but a tragic event amongst a myriad of tragic events. If Jesus did not rise again from the dead, then he cannot be the disabled God because God cannot be contained by death. The resurrection guarantees that the implications of the disabled God are both possible and will be completed. The final chapter will discuss the resurrection of the disabled God.

4

Resurrection

INTRODUCTION

JESUS WAS PHYSICALLY DISABLED during his passion because of his physical weakness and suffering. He also identified with people with intellectual disabilities, by entering into their experience of abandonment, loneliness, poverty, and stigma. Therefore, we can rightly call Jesus the disabled God. However, in calling Jesus the disabled God we must be careful to grasp that he has this title because of the cross, not because he is eternally disabled. On the contrary, Jesus no longer experiences disability since he is risen from the dead. We should not be fooled by the scars of crucifixion that Jesus still carries in his body. These are marks of identification, not disabling wounds. Jesus cannot forget the cross since it defines his authority as the Lamb of God. His followers cannot forget the cross either. Jesus now has a new, glorified body, which is able to do far more than he could do while on earth before his death. He is exalted above all others; his is the name at which every knee must bow. Yet he is still the disabled God because he has experienced what it is to be disabled and he cannot forget that experience.

THE WOUNDS OF THE RESURRECTED CHRIST

Jesus was raised from the dead still bearing the scars from his crucifixion (Luke 24:37–40; John 20:20, 24–27). Some claim these scars imply that Jesus is still disabled in his resurrected state. But Jesus is not disabled any more. The scars are there for a different reason. The first reason for his scars is simply that they identify the risen Jesus as the one who was crucified. Jesus showed his scars to his disciples so that they could be sure that he had actually risen from the dead. It was not some imposter claiming to be Jesus.

The second reason for the scars is the ongoing importance of the cross. The cross of Jesus is not past and done away with; the cross has continuing importance for both Jesus and his disciples. The cross is not undone by the resurrection; it is not an event that is a mere passing phase of Jesus' journey to glory. The resurrection changes the cross into an event that has saving impact on humanity. But the opposite is also true. Without the cross the resurrection cannot be a saving event. The connection between the two is evident in Rom 4:25, "[Jesus] was handed over to death for our trespasses and was raised for our justification." The disciples of Jesus cannot forget the cross. We are reminded of this by the scars on Jesus' hands and feet. To be a follower of Jesus involves taking up the cross (Luke 14:27).

Jesus continues eternally as the Lamb of God, the one "who takes away the sin of the world" (John 1:29b), because he was crucified. This image is present prominently in the book of Revelation. "Then I saw between the throne and the four living creatures and among the elders a Lamb standing as if it had been slaughtered, having seven horns and seven eyes, which are the seven spirits of God sent out into all the earth" (Rev 5:6). Jesus is Lord over the world because of his self-sacrifice on the cross. His power, symbolized by the seven horns, is given as a direct result of that sacrifice. Therefore, Jesus can never forget that he was crucified and he continues to bear the scars.

The scars of crucifixion are quite unique to Jesus. They are not marks of disability, but marks of identity. They mark Jesus as the crucified one even as he is now risen from the dead and unable to die any more. He is the one who died and is now alive forever and ever (Rev 1:18). He is the Lamb who was slain and now reigns from heaven. The scars continually remind believers that the cross was necessary for our salvation and that we too must carry the cross.

THE RESURRECTION BODY OF JESUS

So what is the resurrected body of Jesus like? One passage that can help answer this question is 1 Cor 15. This is where the resurrection of the dead is discussed in the most concentrated form. Here Paul discusses what resurrection bodies will be like in a general sense. He does not discuss Jesus' body in particular, but the resurrection of Jesus and the resurrection of the believer are fundamentally comparable (compare Phil 3:21; Rom 6:8–9, 8:29). Therefore, Paul's description of the resurrection of the dead should give some insight into the nature of the resurrection body of Jesus.

The first aspect of resurrection to note is that it involves both continuity and transformation. The continuity consists in the fact that the present mortal body will be resurrected (1 Cor 15:53; Phil 3:20–21; Rom 8:11). The person who experiences resurrection is continuous with the person who died. There is a historical continuity that joins together the mortal body of the person and the new immortal body. In the new creation we will be ourselves, not someone else.

In contrast to this continuity, there is a radical discontinuity because of the transformation that takes place in the resurrection. The resurrection of the body is by no means like the resuscitation of a dead body or even rejuvenation of old matter. "Flesh and blood cannot inherit the kingdom of God, nor does the perishable inherit the imperishable" (1 Cor 15:50). Resurrection requires a far-reaching transformation of human existence. Everything will change. The body will be radically new and different to what it is like now.

The resurrection body will be a spiritual body in contrast with the present mortal body. In 1 Cor 15:42–54 Paul speaks of the resurrection as a transformation from the physical body to the spiritual body. The two bodies are vitally different. The present physical body is mortal, weak, destructible, and liable to disease, decay, and shame. The spiritual body is the antithesis, being imperishable, glorious, strong, and immortal. Such a body is living and cannot die (Rom 8:11), nor can it become sick or injured. The body of the resurrected Christian will never experience corruption; it will be outwardly magnificent and will possess endless health and vitality.

But we must understand that the spiritual body is not immaterial. It has substance, but its substance is different to the substance of the mortal body. When Paul talks about the spiritual body, he does not mean that the body will be composed of spirit. Rather he is referring to a body governed by the Holy Spirit, who renews the human spirit. The body governed by the Spirit is thus equipped to commune with the heavenly reality. No more will the body be oppressed by all the negative aspects that come with a body subject to death.

The Gospel descriptions of the body of the resurrected Christ are similar in some ways to Paul's description of the believer's resurrection body and add some detail. While there is substantial continuity with his old existence, the body of the risen Jesus has been transformed so that he is no longer bound by the same limitations. Neither matter nor space placed any limits on the risen Christ. He could move through matter—the sealed tomb (Matt 28:2, 6) and closed or even locked doors (John 20:19, 26). He could appear and disappear instantly (although only one disappearance is recorded). Jesus' new mode of existence is characterized by the fact that he has become a "life-giving spirit" (1 Cor 15:45). In this form of existence the spirit is ultimate; Jesus is unhindered by the limitations of time and space and continuously creates new life for both body and spirit. Jesus is truly himself, but in his resurrected state he is more than he was before.

We can now say something about what the risen body of Jesus is like. It is still the body of Jesus, but it is radically transformed. It can no longer die. It is a spiritual body, governed by the Holy Spirit and given glory, honor, strength, and immortality. It is not limited in the ways that the pre-death body was limited. He is able to do far more than he could before his death. His body cannot be disabled.

THE EXALTED STATE OF THE RESURRECTED CHRIST

Not only is Jesus not disabled in his resurrected state, but neither is he humiliated. Jesus was exalted by his resurrection from the dead in contrast to the humiliation of the cross. A crucified Messiah was oxymoron to Jews because a crucified man must be under God's curse (Deut 21:22–23), but the resurrection of Jesus has shown that this verdict is reversed. No longer is Jesus humiliated, but rather he is exalted. The New Testament often alludes to Ps 110:1, "The LORD says to my lord, 'Sit at my right hand until I make your enemies your footstool,'" with reference to Jesus (e.g., Acts 2:34; Eph 1:20, 22; Heb 1:3, 13, 8:1, 10:12). Jesus is now greatly honored and shares the throne with God (Rev 3:21).

The resurrected Jesus has been exalted to the highest place that is possible for a human being. The result of Jesus' obedience was glory for the Father (Phil 2:9–11) and hence the Father has both raised the Son from the dead (Rom 6:4) and given him authority over the whole of creation, so that humanity shall now revere the Son in the same way in which they revere the Father (John 5:23). Because of his obedience Jesus has been exalted by the Father and given the title "Lord." "Every knee shall bow" at his name (Phil 2:10). Jesus has returned to his pre-incarnate glory, but with even greater glory. None of the stigma, shame, or religious vilification that Jesus experienced as a person with a disability is present for him in his glorious resurrected state.

IS THE RISEN JESUS THE DISABLED GOD?

The risen Christ is no longer disabled, but rather the resurrection has transferred the risen Christ into a new reality radically different to the old. The transformed reality of the resurrected Jesus cannot be compared to the reality of mortal humanity. We cannot understand the resurrected Jesus by looking at the way things are in this present age. He has transcended this mortal life and the existence that is governed by the constraints that accompany it. His resurrection has actually transformed reality. If we could understand Jesus' resurrection within our present outlook, then Jesus could again be subject to suffering and death. Such cannot be the case (Heb 9:28).

Jesus is no longer disabled and he will never again be disabled; he has overcome disability in the cross and entered into a life without the effects of mortality and decay. However, Jesus is still the disabled God. He is the God who has gone to the depths of human physical weakness, pain, suffering, and humiliation, and the resurrection does not dissolve that fact. He remains the disabled God and yet he has transcended disability and overcome it. This fact should give hope to all people who experience the constraints, suffering, stigma, and vilification that often accompany a disability.

IMPLICATIONS FOR HOPE

One aspect of the hope of the resurrection from the dead will be the end of disability. Since Jesus the disabled God no longer experiences disability, those who believe in Jesus will not experience disability in their resurrected state either. This is because the followers of Jesus share in his resurrection. And that resurrection takes us into the new age and leaves behind the present evil age.

The resurrection of the believer is vitally connected to the resurrection of Jesus. "If the Spirit of him who raised Jesus from the dead dwells in you, he who raised Christ from the dead will give life to your mortal bodies also through his Spirit that dwells in you" (Rom 8:11). Whatever resurrection life is like for Jesus, it will be like for those who follow him. Although we have borne the image of the man of dust, Adam, we will bear the image of the man of heaven, Jesus (1 Cor 15:49). We will share his glory (Rom 8:17). The implication is that Christians who now experience disability will not experience disability in the resurrection since the risen Jesus is not disabled.

Both resurrections (Jesus' and ours) belong, not to the old, decaying, obsolete age, but to the new eschatological (end of time) age, in which all things become new. The resurrection of the dead belongs to the future new age and cannot be contained within the confines of the present evil age, in which sin reigns. Jesus "gave himself for our sins to set us free from the present evil age" (Gal 1:4). Even the creation itself longs for the resurrection of the dead because it has been subjected to futility (Rom 8:20–21). Therefore, we know that the resurrection of the dead does not involve restoration of the old creation, but rather causes us to enter into the new creation. The resurrection is future and radically different from our present life.

We cannot be fully human until we enter into the future glorious and incorruptible state that comes about in the resurrection of the dead. When all the corruption of our bodies is a thing of the past, then we will be what we are intended to be. Sickness, disease, and disability do not fit within the new creation. They have no place there. This is the hope to which Christians cling, the hope of new bodies that can never become sick or disabled and can never die. Saying that there is no place for disability in the new age does not mean that there is no place for people with disabilities. People with disabilities have a place in the new creation if their trust is in Christ, but their bodily impairments will be a thing of the past. The old physical and mental impairments will not be part of eternity lived in the presence of God. In that state there will only be glory.

CONCLUSION

Jesus can never forget the cross. He has the scars in his hands and feet to continually remind him of that. We can never forget the cross since it has enabled our salvation from sin. Jesus is forever the Lamb of God who has taken away our sins. He is still the disabled God because he can never forget the disability he experienced on the cross. But he is not disabled any more. All the pain, shame, weakness, and disability of the cross are in the past for Jesus. This fact must give us hope. Because Jesus has risen into the new age of glory in the presence of God, there is hope for his disciples that we will also rise to glory with him. In the new age there will be no more disabling conditions. There will be no more stigma and shame. There will be nothing but strength, glory, honor, and immortality. In that wonderful place we will forever worship Jesus the disabled God.

Conclusion

T HE BIBLE CALLS JESUS by many titles: Son of Man (Mark 2:28; Luke 6:22), the Christ (Matt 16:16), the Son of God (John 20:31), King of kings and Lord of lords (Rev 19:16), Prince of Peace (Isa 9:6), Lord of glory (1 Cor 2:8), Lamb of God (John 1:29), and the Lion of the Tribe of Judah (Rev 5:5). But he can also be called the disabled God because of what he has done for people with disabilities, and because he has experienced disability first hand. Disabled God is not a title given to Jesus in the New Testament, but adding to the names of Jesus does not diminish him or take away from the other titles he rightly holds. We can give more glory to Jesus when we explore more of what he has done on behalf of humanity.

The disabled God adds a new dimension to the way Christians understand God's closeness to us in Jesus Christ. God is not distant from the experience of persons with disabilities, but rather he knows what it is like to have multiple physical disabilities, and he has experienced many of the experiences common to persons with intellectual disabilities. Knowing this could change the way in which persons with disabilities relate to God as one who is intimately affected by their disabilities. It should also change the way in which people with disabilities are treated within the church. If God has such present concern for persons with disabilities, then the church must have a similar concern.

Since more than 10 percent of the world's population has a disability, Christians need to have something to say about disability. They also need to be able to credibly speak about God's concern for people with disabilities. I hope that writing this short piece about Jesus the disabled God has contributed to that possibility. I pray that those who read this book will develop a more positive attitude to people living with disability. And I hope that it offers hope to people who live with physical or intellectual limitations and the misguided prejudice of others.